How Do You Live There?

LIVING ON THE OCEAN

Carol Hand

PowerKiDS press

NEW YORK

Published in 2021 by The Rosen Publishing Group, Inc.
29 East 21st Street, New York, NY 10010

Editor: Kristen Susienka
Designer: Rachel Rising

Photo Credits: Cover, p. 1 Rocksweeper/Shutterstock.com; pp. 3,4,6,7,8,10,12,14,15,18,20,21,22,24,26,28,30 ,31,32 (background) Yevhenii Borshosh/Shutterstock.com; p. 5 Designua/Shutterstock.com; p. 7 lassedesignen/ Shutterstock.com; p. 9 Naci Yavuz/Shutterstock.com; p. 10 Gamma-Rapho/ API / Contributor/Getty Images; p. 11 https://upload.wikimedia.org/wikipedia/commons/6/6b/Frol_de_la_mar_in_roteiro_de_malaca.jpeg; p. 13 Mansell / Contributor/ The LIFE Picture Collection/Getty Images; p. 15 Suware Srisomboon/Shutterstock.com; p. 17 Anton Watman/Shutterstock.com; p. 19 A Cotton Photo/Shutterstock.com; p. 21 Alexandros Michailidis/Shutterstock.com; p.22 Pawelec Andrzej/Shutterstock.com; p. 23 andrey_l/Shutterstock.com; p. 25 3000ad/Shutterstock.com; p. 27 PureSolution/Shutterstock.com; p. 29 Dean Drobot/Shutterstock.com; p.30 https://upload.wikimedia.org/ wikipedia/commons/3/33/Limiting_Factor_floating_on_the_surface_of_the_water_after_a_dive_into_the_Puerto_ Rico_Trench.jpg.

Cataloging-in-Publication Data

Names: Hand, Carol.
Title: Living on the ocean / Carol Hand.
Description: New York : PowerKids Press, 2021. | Series: How do you live there?! | Includes glossary and index.
Identifiers: ISBN 9781725316515 (pbk.) | ISBN 9781725316539 (library bound) | ISBN 9781725316522 (6 pack)
Subjects: LCSH: Ocean--Juvenile literature. | Seas--Juvenile literature. | Marine ecology--Juvenile literature.
Classification: LCC GC21.5 H36 2021 | DDC 551.46--dc23

Manufactured in the United States of America

CPSIA Compliance Information: Batch #CSPK20. For further information contact Rosen Publishing, New York, New York at 1-800-237-9932.

Find us on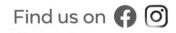

CONTENTS

WHAT ARE OCEANS?

Earth is made up of land and water. In fact, most of the planet is water. Large bodies of water that separate the continents are called oceans. Oceans are made of salt water. All the oceans on Earth are connected to form one huge ocean called the World Ocean, or Global Ocean. Usually, though, maps divide the oceans into five separate oceans: Pacific, Arctic, Atlantic, Indian, and Southern (or Antarctic).

Ocean water collects in huge **basins** on Earth's surface. On average, oceans are 2 miles (3.2 kilometers) deep. The bottoms of ocean basins have mountain ranges and deep ditches called **trenches**. The deepest part of the World Ocean is 7 miles (11 km) deep. It is located in the Pacific Ocean and is called the Mariana Trench.

There are five oceans on Earth, but in reality, they form one big ocean. ⊢————————→

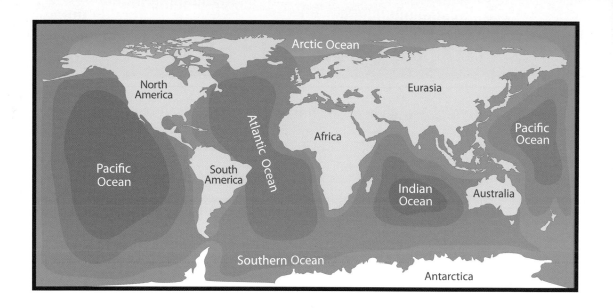

SOUTHERN OCEAN

INDIAN OCEAN

ARCTIC OCEAN

ATLANTIC OCEAN

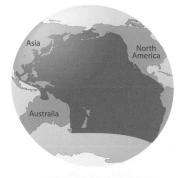

PACIFIC OCEAN

5

HOW OCEANS CHANGE

Oceans are always moving and changing. A few things change the farther down you go in the ocean. Examples are light, temperature, and pressure. Sunlight reaches to about 660 feet (200 meters) below the surface. After that depth, the ocean gets very dark and very cold. The farther down you go, the stronger the pressure from the water will be. Many animals can't live in the ocean's deepest parts because they would be squeezed to death.

The ocean waters change too. **Currents** move water in one direction. This means the ocean water changes and moves all over the world. Some currents are near the ocean's surface. Others are deeper. They move heat around the earth. Wind makes waves. Waves move water and energy around the planet.

Where **coral reefs** live, light reaches to the bottom of the ocean. ⊢—————→

Caribbean Sea

A sea is a smaller part of the ocean mostly surrounded by land. One example is the Caribbean Sea. It is bordered by parts of North, Central, and South America, and by islands. The Caribbean has a tropical climate. This means that it is warm all year round. Many kinds of plants and animals live there. There are whales, dolphins, crocodiles, and sea turtles, as well as coral reefs, where many fish and other animals live. The Caribbean area also has 600 kinds of birds and 13,000 kinds of plants.

EXPLORING THE OCEANS

The first people to explore the oceans around North America were Native Americans. They traveled the ocean by boat. However, they only traveled short distances from land. They went on the ocean to catch fish. They lived in fishing villages on the shores. They fished by diving and by using nets and hooks. Remains of these villages include fish hooks, sinkers, and tools for handling fish nets. They also include spears.

Around the year 1000, Vikings from Europe sailed to North America. Between the 1300s and 1500s, more explorers from Europe started to travel to North and South America. They built large sailing ships to travel across oceans. Early ocean journeys took months or even years. Sailors had to live on their ships. Notable explorers were Ferdinand Magellan and Christopher Columbus.

Ferdinand Magellan planned a journey all the way around the world in the 1500s. ⊢——➤

FERDINAND MAGELLAN

The years 1400 to 1550 are called the Age of Discovery. This is when lots of people began to explore the planet. During this time, two kinds of sailing ships were invented. Caravels were small ships used for exploring. They could stay at sea for a year. Two of Christopher Columbus's ships, the *Niña* and the *Pinta*, were caravels.

Carracks were larger, more powerful ships. They had more sails and could carry bigger crews and more supplies. Carracks were used for war and trading. War cannons could be put on them. Another of Columbus's ships, the *Santa María*, was a carrack.

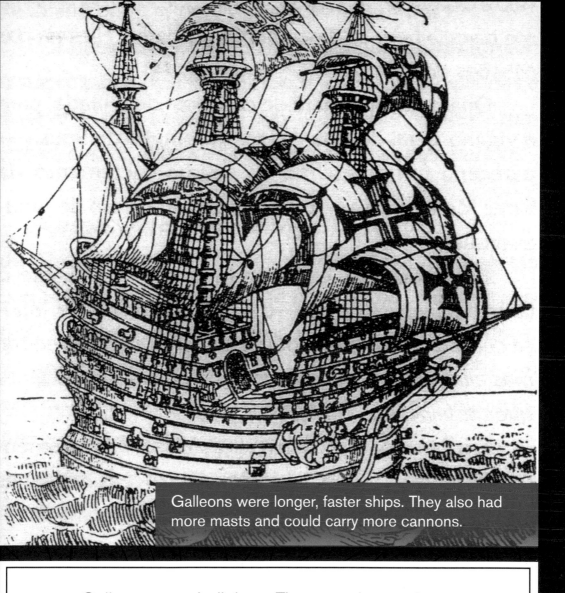

Galleons were longer, faster ships. They also had more masts and could carry more cannons.

Galleons were built later. They were longer than carracks, more narrow, and lower to the water. This made them faster and easier to steer. Galleons were used for war or trading.

A SAILOR'S LIFE AT SEA

A sailor's life on the ocean was dangerous. During a journey, sailors had to climb high in the air to fix or adjust the sails. If they fell, they usually died. This often happened when they worked at night or during stormy weather.

Sailors lived packed together. They slept on the ship's top **deck** on mats. Their sleep was often interrupted. Sailors had almost no fresh food for most of the journey. They often ate hard biscuits called hardtack. They drank water, wine, and beer. A typical meal was salted meat, pea soup, and a hardtack biscuit.

Scurvy is a disease caused by a lack of vitamin C. People usually get vitamin C by eating fruit. At first, scurvy killed many sailors. They didn't have enough fruit to eat. Later, sailors learned to bring more fruit on their journeys.

Anchors at Sea

The anchor holds a ship in place. It is used when the ship is near land or during storms. Most anchors are kept in the bow, or front, of the ship. When the anchor is down, the bow will face into the wind and waves. This is much safer than facing away from them. Early anchors were made of stone. Modern anchors are heavy steel.

A Dutch ship is unloaded after arriving in New Amsterdam (now New York City) in the mid-1600s.

13

LIVING ON THE OCEAN NOW

Today, some people live on floating villages or in boat communities. Some examples are found in Asia. Several of these villages are built on tall stilts. The people live very simply. They survive by fishing and tourism. Some countries with floating villages are Cambodia, Thailand, and the Philippines.

People in the navy live for months on large ships called **aircraft carriers**. They are powered by **nuclear reactors**. Between 5,000 and 6,000 people can live on an aircraft carrier for months. It has galleys, or kitchens, and cafeterias called mess halls, where meals are cooked and served. There are stores for buying supplies, and doctors and dentists live and work on board. People also take vacations on cruise liners, which are large ships with lots of fun activities to do.

These boats in Thailand are part of the world's best-known floating market.

Getting Fresh Water at Sea

Humans cannot drink salt water. They need fresh water to survive. People who live on the ocean are no different. One way to get fresh water is to catch and store rainwater. Modern ships and boats have rain collectors. On small ships, awnings or sun covers may be set up to send rainwater into jugs or tanks. Rain is the best source of fresh water. Watermakers are another source. These machines remove salt and germs from ocean water. This makes the water safe to drink.

LIFE ABOARD

Life on an aircraft carrier is different than life on land. Talking to friends and family is more challenging. There is no cell signal or Wi-Fi. Satellite Internet is very slow. Living spaces are also close together. Everyone shares a bathroom, gym, and television.

People on an aircraft carrier do many jobs. Some keep the carrier running, others cook the meals, and others fly and take care of aircraft. People who work below deck can go days or weeks without seeing sunlight. On the flight deck, it's loud and dangerous. Jets take off and land.

Living on a cruise liner is similar to living on an aircraft carrier. Connection with people back on land is minimal. However, there are more restaurants and fun activities to do on a cruise ship.

Cruise ships are great fun for tourists. Some people want to turn them into permanent ocean homes. ⊢——→

Life on an Oil Rig

Another unique way of life is happening on oil rigs in the ocean. These areas are places where oil is being drilled from the bottom of the sea. Nearly 200 people can live on one oil rig. Living on an oil rig has challenges and benefits. Rig workers are far away from family and friends, but they can communicate with Internet access on board. There are also TVs, movie theaters, and fresh food on site. People work 12-hour shifts at any time of day or night.

THREATS FACING OCEAN LIVING

Earth's oceans face many problems today. Some threats include water pollution, **global warming**, and **climate change**. Water pollution is when litter or waste (food or items left behind by humans) is put into the water. This makes the water dirty and hurts animals and plants in the water. It is one of the main problems for oceans today.

Global warming is the process by which harmful chemicals and gases are released into the air by factories, cars, and other vehicles. These gases trap heat in the atmosphere, warming Earth. A lot of the extra heat ends up in the oceans. Rising water temperatures make life harder for some ocean plants and animals. Over time, warmer ocean temperatures can also cause changes in weather patterns on land. Strong storms, droughts, or other natural disasters are common with climate change.

Global warming is dangerous to coral reefs. This coral reef has lost all its algae because it's too warm. Without algae, the corals die.

There are many people fighting climate change around the world today. Leaders include Green Peace, young activist Greta Thunberg, and the United Nations. There have been many efforts by countries around the world to reduce their **carbon footprint**. Some examples are the Kyoto Protocol of 1997 and the Paris Climate Agreement of 2015. Most of the world signed both of these agreements, vowing to help protect Earth's environment.

Building more communities on the ocean could also help fight global warming. People living on the ocean would be more likely to want to protect it. They would also likely be willing to live more simply, or use **renewable energy** sources to make electricity. They would also likely educate others about life on the oceans, and life in the oceans.

More people around the world are stressing the need to protect the environment. |⎯⎯⎯⎯⟶

Melting Worlds

In the 21st century, global warming is affecting the oceans in a big way. Increasing Earth's temperature is warming and melting some of the planet's coldest places. Glaciers in Antarctica, the coldest place on Earth, are melting. Adding more water to Earth's oceans means ocean waters rise. Rising ocean waters can lead to flooding in places near a country's coast. As waters rise, more people will need to learn how to live on the ocean.

THE FUTURE OF OCEAN LIFE

Some people want to build floating cities or colonies on the ocean (photo below). Others want to build cities *underneath* the ocean (photo to the right). One reason is the population is growing. If we can't live on other planets, maybe we can live elsewhere on our planet.

Another reason is to cut down on ocean pollution. Ocean cruises hurt the environment because they burn diesel or gas fuel. This causes air pollution. They also dump human waste into the oceans. This hurts plants and animals. Other large ships do the same. Ocean cities would stay in one

These pictures (left and right) are designs for possible future ocean living. Ocean structures could float while being anchored to the ocean bottom.

place and could prevent some of this pollution. They would not burn oil or gas. They would likely use renewable energy, like solar and wind energy, for electricity, and they would recycle waste.

Some ocean cities could use existing ocean structures, like cruise liners, for their city. Oil rigs could become hotels or apartments. One new idea is called Oceanix City. Each community would be built on large floating platforms. There would be room for 300 to 10,000 people. Each platform would be connected to the seafloor in shallow water. Walkways would link multiple platforms together. The community would be environmentally friendly. Greenhouses and underwater gardens would grow food. The platforms would also use water and recycled waste for power.

Another design is the floating **ecopolis**, or the Lilypad. It would produce more energy than it uses and recycle most of its waste. It could potentially support many types of plants and animals. It would use solar, wind, and water energy.

Another ocean city of the future might look like this.

CREATING ISLANDS

Some modern ideas are actually happening now. Coastal countries are building new islands. These fake islands are built of sand from the ocean floor. They can create new land to help crowded cities expand, or grow. They can also be used for businesses and homes.

Dubai's Palm Islands are one example. They were made to be shaped like a palm tree. There is a curved island above the tree, like a crescent moon. These new islands add land and beaches. Tourists can visit them. The islands have businesses and some homes, but they may not last long. Some are sinking back into the ocean.

Underwater Resorts

Hydropolis and Poseidon are underwater resort hotels. Hydropolis is near Dubai, in the United Arab Emirates. When completed, it will be the world's first underwater hotel. It will be 60 feet (18 m) below sea level. It will have a shopping mall and a system to defend against attacks. Poseidon will be built in the Pacific island country of Fiji. It will be smaller than Hydropolis. Visitors to Poseidon will be able to see beautiful coral reefs.

This is the city of Dubai, on the Persian Gulf. In the water are "fronds" from the Palm Islands that have been built to add living space.

WHAT CAN YOU DO?

Many people are excited about living on or under the ocean. They like the idea of being by water all the time and growing their own food in an environmentally friendly way. Ocean cities could help more people live on Earth. They could also help battle problems like global warming. There are many ideas being thought of every day. Some will happen, while others will be replaced by even newer and cooler ideas. Ocean cities may be the wave of the future!

You can do a lot to help others understand how important the oceans are. Think of some ways you can make a difference for the oceans. Could you recycle more? Pollute less? Tell your friends about the dangers the ocean faces? Any way you can help will make a difference.

People clear plastic from a beach so it will not enter the water and harm ocean life. ⊢⟶

5 DEEPEST TRENCHES IN THE 5 OCEANS

OCEAN	TRENCH	DEPTH
Arctic	Molloy Trench	18,209 feet (5,550 m)
Atlantic	Puerto Rico Trench	27,480 feet (8,376 m)
Indian	Java Trench	23,596 feet (7,192 m)
Pacific	Mariana Trench	36,201 feet (11,033 m)
Southern	South Sandwich Trench	24,389 feet (7,434 m)

PUERTO RICO TRENCH

GLOSSARY

aircraft carrier: A huge navy ship from which jet fighters take off and land.

basin: A bowl-like structure that holds water; for example, an ocean basin.

carbon footprint: A person's output of carbon dioxide into the environment due to activities like traveling by car, bus, train, or airplane. Carbon dioxide in the atmosphere contributes to global warming.

carrack: A sailing ship larger than a caravel, used for warfare or trading.

climate change: The process by which weather patterns change due to the effects of global warming.

coral reef: A colorful underwater environment that stretches along the seafloor and is home to many sea creatures, including animals called corals.

current: The movement of ocean water from one place to another.

deck: The top part of a ship where people walk around.

ecopolis: A combination of "ecology" and "metropolis," meaning an environmentally friendly city.

global warming: The process by which Earth's global temperature rises due to harmful gases being put into the air.

nuclear reactor: A structure that produces power using a process called fission.

renewable energy: Power that is produced without hurting the environment, such as from the sun, wind, or waves.

trench: A deep ditch. Trenches form the deepest parts of the oceans.

INDEX

WEBSITES

Due to the changing nature of Internet links, PowerKids Press has developed an online list of websites related to the subject of this book. This site is updated regularly. Please use this link to access the list:
www.powerkidslinks.com/hdylt/ocean